**Parl**

## CHATTO
### CounterBlasts

Adam
# LIVELY

# Parliament:
# The Great British
# Democracy Swindle

Chatto & Windus
LONDON

Published in 1990 by
Chatto & Windus Ltd
20 Vauxhall Bridge Road
London SW1V 2SA

A CIP catalogue record for this book
is available from the British Library

ISBN 0 7011 3641 3

Photoset in Linotron Ehrhardt by
Rowland Phototypesetting Ltd
Bury St Edmunds, Suffolk
Printed in Great Britain by
St Edmundsbury Press Ltd
Bury St Edmunds, Suffolk

WE LIVE IN the days of democracy. From South Africa to Estonia, people power has made itself felt, and for a moment at least it has seemed as though the world is moving towards freedom and democracy and away from authoritarianism. Ideological fictions have crumbled, bureaucracies have been swept away. But in Britain we always seem to be moving in the other direction. How is it possible, in a 'democracy', for a government to ramrod into law a measure as massively unpopular, as manifestly unjust and bureaucratic, as the poll tax? It is the imposition of ideology on an almost Romanian scale. The answer lies in part, of course, in the fanaticism of the Prime Minister and her advisors. But her fanaticism would be comparatively harmless were it not for the enormous power that our political system hands to her on a plate. It is time, in this new democratic age, that we asked some fundamental questions about our own 'democracy' – our unwritten constitution, our voting system, our 'Mother of Parliaments'. Could it be that what we need is not just a change of government, but a complete change of system?

In the euphoric days of November 1989, when

I

the Berlin Wall was coming down, Denis Healey sounded a note of warning in the *Observer*:

> The revolution in Eastern Europe, as in the Soviet Union, is in part a revolution for national independence ... [But] independence is no answer to national feeling when the boundaries of potential nation states enclose powerful minorities which want independence as much as the majorities. Britain has learnt this in Northern Ireland as well as Spain in the Basque country, and Azerbaijan in Nagorno Karabakh.
>
> The most important challenge facing mankind after the end of the Cold War is to devise new political structures which will accommodate such national feelings. These structures must also be compatible with the new international economic and financial structures created by modern technology.

The historical background to Denis Healey's fears is the ethnic patchwork of Central and Eastern Europe, the jumble of states that played such an important part in causing two world wars. Ethnic pluralism and political nationalism have formed an explosive and catastrophic mixture in the twentieth century. The adoption of the simplistic doctrine of 'national self-determination' at the Versailles Conference of 1919 created more problems than it solved. In the 1930s, the existence of German-speaking minorities within the newly established states of Central Europe provided a justification for Nazi expansionism. A truly democratic reconstruction of contemporary Europe requires the creation of new institutions for resolving conflict: institutions that bypass the old rigidities of nationalism, and that can provide mechanisms for democratic control over those economic and environmental forces that now recognise no frontiers. What Chernobyl demonstrated above all else was the inadequacy for the modern world of the doctrines of national sovereignty and national self-determination.

We in Britain are in no way detached from the need for a democratic reconstruction of Europe. It is tempting but short-sighted to see the democratic revolutions of Central and Eastern Europe as simply a process of 'them' coming over to 'us', the Western democracies. (Mrs Thatcher even seems to think that they are coming over to join the British Conservative Party.) But in the longer term, once the ugly note of triumphalism has died away, the question is bound to arise: How democratic are *we*?

The Cold War was a rigidity of the mind as much as of international relations. It was easy for Western politicians to fall back on the dualism of 'dictatorship' versus 'democracy': 'We live in a democracy, they live under a dictatorship.' We gazed at the glassy, frozen surface of Eastern Europe under Stalinism and saw only the reflection of our self-satisfied selves: 'We live in a democracy.' Now that the world of illusion is shattered, old questions begin to acquire new force. Are some 'democracies' more democratic than others? What criteria should we use in judging how democratic a society is?

To ask such basic questions in a British context goes against the grain. British politicians of Left and Right have tended to adhere to the kind of institutional conservatism which found its most famous exponent in the late eighteenth-century philosopher and politician Edmund Burke. Burke, pointing to the bloody example of the French Revolution, argued that it was dangerous to alter the institutions of government merely on the basis of abstract considerations of principle. For later politicians, this pragmatic philosophy has become an excuse for 'muddling through'. One of the great strengths of our unwritten constitution, it is said, is its flexibility. British politicians have traditionally seen that flexibility as sufficient to meet any particular problem, and have taken our constitution's longevity as an argument for its continued usefulness, not its redundancy. 'It is with infinite caution,' writes Burke in his *Reflections on the Revolution in France*, 'that any man ought to venture upon pulling down an edifice which has answered in any tolerable degree for ages the common purposes of society, or on building it up again without having models or patterns of approved utility before his eyes.' The analogy is drawn between the British constitution and some magnificent, weathered old building (perhaps Charles Barry's neo-Gothic pile, the Palace of Westminster, drifts into the mind at this point, though that is not nearly as old as it pretends to be). Pride in this ancient pile has traditionally been a source of solidarity for British politicians of all persuasions. As Aneurin Bevan put it in the last speech he ever gave: 'I believe that this country of ours ... is being looked on by the rest of the world as the custodian of democratic representative government.'

Thirty years later, of course, that pride has worn a little thin. Are the British still looked on as custodians of democratic, open government? The ban, announced without notice by the Home Secretary in October 1988, on broadcast interviews with members or 'supporters' of Sinn Fein and other named organisations, created world-wide interest. President Botha was moved to say that he would consider similar measures in South Africa. That is the kind of example we set now.

The concerted campaign by the government to censor and intimidate the press and broadcasters; the wide new powers that have been given to the police under the Public Order Act (1986) – which severely infringes the fundamental democratic right to freedom of assembly – and the Police and Criminal Evidence Act (1984); the restriction of freedom of movement through exclusion orders preventing people (without trial or proper right of appeal) from travelling between Northern Ireland and the rest of the United Kingdom; the introduction of legislation that discriminates against ethnic and other minorities under the British Nationality Act (1981) and Section 28 of the Local Government Act (1988). All this has become a familiar litany of complaint against the Conservative governments that have ruled us since 1979. But how have these infringements of basic civil liberties been allowed to happen? What can be done to rectify them and ensure that they don't happen again?

For many on the Left, of course, the answer is obvious. The problem is Thatcher, and the solution is to get her out and put the Labour Party in. Nothing should distract from that essential task. Once Mr Kinnock is installed in Number 10, Britain will, through the beneficence of Labour Party policies, become a land of justice and wholly enlightened government. Yet surely such faith is naive. The Labour Party is not an assembly of saints, and past Labour governments have not been above introducing authoritarian or discriminatory legislation. The Prevention of Terrorism Act, whose provision for detention without charge for up to seven days has been condemned by the European Commission on Human Rights, was originally introduced in 1974 by a Labour Home Secretary,

6

Roy Jenkins (who himself described the measures as 'draconian'). The 1968 Commonwealth Immigrants Act was, as the Labour government that introduced it accepted, racially motivated – designed to keep out East African Asians. R.H.S. Crossman, a member of that Labour cabinet, later acknowledged that the legislation 'would have been declared unconstitutional in any country with a written constitution and a Supreme Court'.

The Labour Party has now taken the significant step of recognising in principle that special provision is needed for the safeguarding of civil liberties. In January 1990 they published a 'Charter of Rights', a proposal for four specific bills designed to protect freedom of information, sexual and racial equality, equal access to law, and privacy. Furthermore, a new directly elected second chamber would replace the House of Lords and have the power (though no obligation) to delay for the term of one parliament any legislation that contravened these bills. No timetable has yet been forthcoming on when a Labour government would make these changes, and one may be forgiven for suspecting that they will remain merely vague promises designed to deflect criticism. But even if one takes Labour's commitment at face value, the measures proposed are, as we shall see, exactly the kind of conservative muddling-through of which Burke might have approved. They do not amount to anything like a proper protection of civil liberties because, quite apart from the selectivity of the rights to be protected, they do not recognise the fundamental issue – the need for a written constitution to curb the power of parliament. To understand why a written constitution is needed – and to understand how Mrs Thatcher's authoritarian government has been able to get away with what it has – it is necessary to ask some fundamental questions about the nature of democracy.

For an Athenian of the fifth century BC, democracy consisted in the citizens of the city meeting together in person, debating and voting on matters of common concern. There is much that is attractive in that simple vision, and it remains at the heart of modern democratic theory: decisions should be made on the basis of the will of the majority. Many people have advocated that rather than hand over debating and voting to representatives, we should return to Athenian-style direct or 'participatory' democracy. But Athenian democracy was in many ways very restricted. Citizenship was in effect an inherited privilege, limited to a minority of the adult population – women, resident 'foreigners' and slaves were excluded. The result was that the body of voters was small and homogeneous. Basic questions ('Should slavery be abolished?' for example, or 'What rights should women have?') that might have caused irrevocable splits between groups of voters if the franchise had been wider, could be decided without a clash of interests or simply kept off the agenda.

In the eighteenth century, Jean-Jacques Rousseau argued that smallness and homogeneity were essential preconditions for real, that is participatory, democracy. But the world we live in now is one of large nation-states with diverse populations (and, increasingly, one of supra-national bodies in which the range of interests is even wider). In these circumstances, the Athenian model is clearly inadequate. Quite apart from the need for representation, there is the problem of how minorities are to be included in the democratic process. Take the simplest example, of a society made up of two sectarian groups, A and B, who see their interests as clashing fundamentally. (Following Denis Healey's examples, one could substitute for A and B Northern Irish Protestants and Catholics, Spaniards and Basques, or Azeris and Armenians.) Assuming that they are not exactly equal in size – the proportions could be as close as 51 per cent as against 49 per cent – one group will find itself in a permanent minority. If decisions are based simply on the will of a bare majority, it will in effect be excluded from the decision-making process. Could such a society be called a democracy? And what happens if, through a 'democratic' vote of the majority, a minority's democratic rights are removed?

9

What if, for the sake of argument, the Conservative government decided to deny those who couldn't pay their poll tax the right to vote? Or what if they decided to pursue the logic of Clause 28 a stage further, and deny completely the right of freedom of speech to those who tolerate 'the acceptability of homosexuality as a pretended family relationship'? Could Britain still be called a 'democracy' in those circumstances?

This basic problem of majorities using the machinery of 'democratic' decision-making to exercise a tyranny over minorities (or in some circumstances – under our electoral system, for example – it could be a minority tyrannising over another minority, or a majority) has long been recognised. Aristotle advocated a system of 'mixed' government in which the democratic component was balanced by entrenched aristocratic and monarchical elements. In the eighteenth century, Baron de Montesquieu saw in the British constitution, with its king, lords and commons, the perfect embodiment of Aristotle's ideal of mixed or balanced government.

Neither Aristotle nor Montesquieu were democrats. (The Britain of the eighteenth century that Montesquieu so admired, with its electorate of about 2 per cent of the adult population, was not a democracy.) But it would be wrong to see the problem of majority tyrannies as a fatal flaw in the whole idea of democracy. The aim of democracy is to achieve as just and equitable a distribution of political power as possible. So a system that allows any group to be unjustly discriminated against in the distribution of power (denying it the right to vote, for example, or to free speech or free assembly, which are essential in order to participate in the democratic process) is no longer a democracy. In answer to the question posed earlier, if the government denied the vote to people who hadn't paid their poll tax, or denied homosexuals the right to free speech, Britain would no longer be a democracy. South Africa – no matter how exemplary the polls it carries out among the white population – is not a democracy, because it denies blacks the right to vote.

So securing the equal rights of all groups in society, and preventing one group (be it a majority or minority) from tyrannising over other groups, is not a curtailment of democracy, but essential to it. Following on from Aristotle's vision of 'mixed' or 'balanced' government, political thinkers in the eighteenth century – in what is usually called the 'republican' tradition – devised ways in which constitutional checks and balances could be built into a democratic system so that no single group or interest could gain untrammelled power over the rest of society. For James Madison, one of the 'Founding Fathers' who drew up the American constitution, 'Among the numerous advantages promised by a well-constructed union, none deserves to be more accurately developed than its tendency to break and control the violence of faction.' These checks and balances can take the form of Bills of Rights (with mechanisms for judicial review to invalidate any legislation that contravenes the rights); the strict separation of legislature, executive and judiciary, with their respective powers written and closely defined; and a similar division of powers between central and regional government. The purpose of such checks and balances is to disperse power, to prevent it from being concentrated in one body, in order that any decision should have as wide a consent as possible. A Bill of Rights, enforceable through the courts, protects the basic democratic rights of even the smallest minority group (ultimately, the individual). This approach to government recognises that society is pluralistic, that it is made up of a great range of groups, each of whose interests and rights should be respected. It differs fundamentally from the model derived from the Athenian example, which holds simply that the will of the bare majority should prevail. The one approach to government we could call 'pluralistic' or 'consensual', the other 'majoritarian' or 'majority-ruled'.

Such basic considerations concerning democracy may seem far removed from the workings of day-to-day politics, but they can help us to judge whether some 'democracies' are in fact more democratic than others. Arend Lijphart, a political scientist, has studied twenty-one democratic countries from the point of view of the 'pluralistic' and 'majoritarian' models outlined above, placing them on a scale from the most pluralistic to the most majority-ruled. He gives eight defining characteristics of an extreme 'majoritarian' system:

– the concentration of executive power in the hands of one party
– a lack of separation between executive and legislature
– a unicameral legislature, or at least a legislature in which power is heavily weighted in favour of one 'House'
– a two-party system
– a party system which is aligned along one set of issues (aligned along differences in social and economic policy, for example)
– a 'first-past-the-post' electoral system (Lijphart describes this as 'a perfect embodiment of the majoritarian philosophy')
– a unitary and centralised government
– an unwritten constitution and parliamentary sovereignty

Invert all these elements (executive 'power-sharing' or coalition, a multi-party system, proportional representation, federalism rather than centralised government etc.) and you will have the extreme pluralist model. Lijphart's twenty-one countries are ranged along the scale between these two extremes. The USA, for example, has some majoritarian features (the concentration of executive power in the hands of the president, a two-party system, first-past-the-post voting for most elections) but rather more pluralistic features (separation of executive and legislature, a bicameral legislature, federalism and a written constitution).

The eight defining characteristics of an extreme majority-ruled system will sound all too familiar to a British reader. Lijphart himself refers to it as 'the Westminster model'. If we imagine Lijphart's twenty-one countries stretched out on a line, with the most pluralist on the extreme left (Switzerland and Belgium, according to Lijphart) and the most majoritarian on the extreme right, then we find Britain way out on the right wing. We are not quite on our own – of all the democracies studied by Lijphart, only New Zealand is more majoritarian than Britain. But one should bear in mind that New Zealand is a much smaller and more homogeneous country than Britain. (The only respect in which New Zealand deviates from the majority-ruled model is that its electoral system is modified to guarantee representation to its major ethnic minority, the Maoris.)

The purpose of these international comparisons is not to argue that we should suddenly become like Switzerland and Belgium, or even the United States, but simply to point out how eccentric our political system is. So dominated is our daily political life by the clash of steel in the two-party battle, that it is difficult sometimes to remember how out of step we are with other countries in terms of the structures within which that party battle is fought. Among Lijphart's democracies, only Britain, New Zealand and Israel have no form of written constitution. For many people, this uniqueness is a source of pride. As Dickens' Mr Podsnap famously expressed it: 'This Island was blest, Sir, to the Direct Exclusion of such Other Countries as – as there may happen to be.' While the mere fact that our political system is unusual is not in itself an argument against it, it might at least give us pause for thought.

Taken in turn, Arend Lijphart's eight characteristics of a majoritarian system provide an almost complete definition of the way we are governed:

*Concentration of executive power in the hands of one party.* Coalition government is not in fact completely alien to British traditions – there were a number during the period 1914–45 – but there have been none since the Second World War. The short-lived 'Lib-Lab Pact' of 1977–78 was not a genuine coalition, since it did not give Liberals seats in the cabinet. Politicians of the two major parties dismiss the idea of coalitions on two grounds – that they make for 'weak' or 'unstable' government, and that they result in the elector not knowing what s/he is voting for (because their party will subsequently make deals with other parties). The first argument studiously ignores the many stable democracies in Europe that are regularly governed by coalitions. It is particularly paradoxical to hear Labour politicians bewailing with one breath the fact that we have an authoritarian government, and giving dire warning with the next of the dangers of 'weak' and 'unstable' government. The second point is somewhat disingenuous. What government has ever fulfilled all its manifesto commitments? The two major parties are themselves coalitions of individuals with a variety of interests and opinions, between which agreement is often reached in private. The essential process would be no different with coalition government, except that it would become rather more public and democratically accountable.

Defenders of the British political system often point to the virtues of 'cabinet government'. Behind the closed doors of the cabinet room, so the theory goes, government policy is hammered out through a free and frank exchange of views. Mrs Thatcher has demonstrated the naivety of this faith in cabinet government. Any Minister who expresses an independent view quickly becomes only a 'semi-detached' member of the government, and is then axed – if he hasn't already fallen on his sword. Peter Hennessy, the writer on Whitehall matters, has aptly described Mrs Thatcher's cabinets as governed by 'the politics of the abattoir'.

*Lack of separation between executive and legislature.* Another cornerstone of the British system is the principle of 'ministerial accountability'. Ministers have to answer directly to parliament for their actions, and ultimately parliament can vote a government out of office. Faith in the ability of parliament to exercise this magisterial power over government reaches into all corners of political life. In his *Arguments for Democracy*, for example, Tony Benn assures us that despite all the powers that have accrued to governments in recent decades, 'The ultimate power of the House of Commons to topple a prime minister remains unaffected . . . The very fact that these powers are there operates to restrict and restrain the exercise of power by premiers and ministers.' This is surely even more credulous than a faith in cabinet government. Only once since the Second World War, in 1979, has a government been brought down by a vote of the House of Commons. Such is the power of party discipline in this country that once a government is installed with an overall majority in the House of Commons, it is highly unlikely to be removed. The theory is that parliament exercises control over the government; in practice, power flows in the opposite direction. Mrs Thatcher, through her Whips, keeps a tight rein on her parliamentary party. Ministerial preferment can be withdrawn from anyone who steps out of line. And there is no reason to think that a Labour Prime Minister would act any differently. With few exceptions, Members of Parliament vote not as independent overseers of the government, but as party members. The point is amply expressed by Michael Foot, in his *Loyalists and Loners*, during the course of a panegyric to Enoch Powell: 'He understood . . . so much better than all the exponents of consensus and coalition politics, that allegiance to party is the essential ingredient of the British political system.'

There has been one notable attempt in recent years to improve parliamentary scrutiny of government. In 1980, fourteen Departmental Select Committees were set up to monitor government activity in various areas. Some parliamentary committees are more successful than others – the Public Accounts Committee (originally set up by Gladstone in 1866), with the back-up it gets from the National Audit Office, has been particularly effective in bringing issues to public attention – but one has only to remember Kenneth Clarke's contemptuous dismissal of criticism from the Select Committee on Agriculture of his handling of the salmonella in eggs affair to realise how weak the committee system remains as an instrument for controlling government.

*Power heavily weighted in favour of one House of the legislature.* Britain is the only democracy in the world that still retains an element of aristocratic, hereditary government. Clearly, the House of Lords as it presently exists has no place in a modern democracy. Many in the Labour Party would like to see it abolished without any replacement, creating a unicameral legislature. Indeed, the proposals for a new second chamber that have come out of the party's policy review would deprive it of the powers that the House of Lords presently has to delay money bills for one month and other bills for a year. The sole effective power that the proposed new chamber would have would be that of delaying legislation that touched on the four 'Rights' bills. Thus Labour's proposals are, if anything, a move in the majoritarian direction.

*A two-party system, aligned primarily along one set of issues, and elected by a first-past-the-post voting system.* These characteristics of our party and electoral system are clearly interrelated. With proportional representation, we would no longer have what is in effect a two-party system. The two parties take their basic and familiar stances on the same socioeconomic issues. Minor parties that try to introduce different forms of alignment ('green' versus 'grey', or regionalism versus centralism, for example) are denied fair representation and squeezed out by the electoral system.

*A unitary and centralised government.* British local government has a tradition of exercising wide powers – but because these powers have never been guaranteed or protected, they can be easily clawed back to the centre. The most striking example of this paradox is the government of Northern Ireland between 1921 and 1972. During that period, Stormont in effect exercised all the powers of a central government (except defence and foreign affairs), only to find itself abolished, and direct rule from Westminster imposed, in March 1972. Over the past ten years, Thatcher has exploited this power of Westminster to remove local government. In 1985 the Greater London Council and the metropolitan authorities were abolished despite local opposition. Greater central control of local government has been exercised through rate-capping, manipulation of the rate-support grant, and 'charge-capping' associated with the poll tax. Again, we are out of step with European developments. In recent years the trend in France, Italy and Spain has been towards greater decentralisation and greater powers for regional governments.

West Germany, of course, already has a highly decentralised federal system under its post-war constitution.

*Parliamentary sovereignty and an unwritten constitution.* The principle of parliamentary sovereignty is the key to understanding what is wrong with the British politics, the conceptual cornerstone that upholds the whole ancient pile. A.V. Dicey, in the bible of English constitutional law, *Law of the Constitution* (1885), defines it like this:

> The principle of Parliamentary sovereignty means neither more nor less than this, namely that Parliament . . . has, under the English constitution, the right to make or unmake any law whatever; and further, that no person or body is recognised by the law of England as having a right to override or set aside the legislation of Parliament.

The extreme majoritarianism and anti-pluralism of the principle of parliamentary sovereignty is obvious. Any party that gains an overall majority in the House of Commons (and under the first-past-the-post electoral system that need not – and rarely does – mean a majority of the electorate) can in theory do what it likes. If a group is small enough or carries little political weight – homosexuals, for example, or 'hippies', or the unemployed, or immigrants – the government (which, it should be remembered, has the support of a *minority* of the electorate) can deprive that minority group of many basic civil rights. One could not imagine a more striking instance of a system in which one group is given the power to tyrannise over others.

In defence of the present system, it can be argued that governments have to answer to the electorate at election time. That is what stops us becoming a dictatorship. Secondly, no matter what the theory may be, there are certain things that a government just could not get away with in a basically civilised and democratic society like ours. The first point puts too much faith in a cross made on a piece of paper once every five years. One can easily imagine a situation in which a voter may feel a vague unease about the reports s/he has been hearing about the government's treatment of (or the opposition's policies on) homosexuals, or the unemployed, or immigrants, but decides to set those misgivings aside and mark the ballot paper according to where the parties stand on taxation, or the environment, or whatever the voter's own political priority may be. The voter may be insufficiently informed, or the problem may feel sufficiently distant from his/ her everyday concerns, to make it more of a political priority. An election every five years, in short, is far too blunt an instrument with which to protect the rights of minorities.

The second point is based on an argument that runs something like this: Britain could never become an uncivilised and undemocratic country because it is a civilised and democratic country. We will meet this kind of inane circularity again in considering objections to a radical reform of our political system. This feeling is, I suspect, based on a hope that, deep down, the 'postwar consensus' still exists, that the problem of the past ten years has been one of 'Thatcherism', and that once she is gone that consensus will magically reassert itself. This is not good enough. The future is pressing in on us: with the Cold War over, the only safe prediction that can be made is that Europe is about to undergo a period of rapid political and economic change. Who can foretell what new forms of authoritarianism – Left or Right, grey or green, European or British – the next fifty years may throw up? In these circumstances, it is dangerous merely to trust in some mystical notion of 'British tolerance'. It is certainly true that without an active consensus of politicians and citizens behind it, written constitutions and Bills of Rights become no more than vacuous pieties. Many dictatorships – as opponents of reform never fail to point out – have had exemplary written constitutions. This may demonstrate that a written constitution is not in itself a sufficient guarantee of democracy and liberty, but it doesn't answer the argument that it may be a necessary one. Part of the problem in this country is that there is no strong and distinct tradition of public law, of law governing the relationship between the individual and government. We lack the language with which to defend ourselves, as individuals or as members of minority groups, against the claims of the majority and the state. A written constitution would serve an important educative function, through the courts and through schools, universities and the media, in providing citizens with that language. It could help to shore up the British 'consensus' where it has fallen into disrepair, rebuild it where it has completely collapsed, and even create it where it never existed in the first place.

A written constitution, and hence the ending of parliamentary sovereignty, is the *sine qua non* of any radical reform of our political system. If, as I have tried to argue, the aim of democracy is to distribute political power as widely and equitably as possible, then the principle of parliamentary sovereignty – which concentrates supreme power in a single body – is, in an important sense, undemocratic. Any reform that attempts to guard our liberties while hanging on to the principle of parliamentary sovereignty will be seriously flawed. The Labour Party's proposals for constitutional reform, for example, suffer from precisely this defect. They propose that their four 'Rights' Bills would be 'entrenched' by giving the new second chamber power to delay any legislation affecting them for the term of one parliament. In effect this is not a proper constitutional check at all, since it assumes the somewhat unlikely situation of the party that has a majority in the House of Commons being in a minority in the second chamber. There would be no constitutional *obligation* on the second chamber to delay legislation. Furthermore, there would be nothing to stop a future government simply repealing the original legislation that gave the second chamber the delaying power.

Despite Labour's frequent expressions of horror at the idea of the courts getting involved in politics, the method of 'entrenching' legislation it proposes would not actually obviate the need for a form of judicial review. Given the unlikely circumstance of the second chamber challenging the government, disputes would inevitably arise as to whether a particular Bill did in fact bear on the rights legislation. (The present government, for example, has argued that Clause 28 is nothing to do with freedom of speech or discrimination against homosexuals, but is merely a matter concerning local government expenditure.) And who would settle such disputes? It could not be the government, or they would be acting as judge and jury in their own case. Presumably it would have to be a supreme court, of exactly the kind that the proposal to 'entrench' the legislation in a second chamber (rather than in a written constitution) was originally designed to avoid. In general, Labour's proposals for constitutional reform as they stand at present are so contradictory that one must doubt whether they are serious proposals for action.

The Labour Party is being dragged only very slowly towards the realisation that there may be something fundamentally wrong with our political system. The Conservatives – except for a handful of individuals like Sir Edward Gardner, who introduced a Human Rights Bill in 1986 – ignore the subject completely. People who advocate a written constitution, proportional representation or other structural reforms of our political system are dismissed by politicians of Left and Right as middle-class dreamers hopelessly out of touch with 'real' issues – as though having a view about our political system precluded a concern about education or the health service. Mr Kinnock has referred to such people as 'whiners, wingers and wankers'. But then this was exactly the kind of attitude that was taken not so long ago by the very same politicians to those funny people in sandals who were always banging on about the environment . . .

If the arguments against our present political system are so convincing, how does one explain the depth of attachment to it? Of course, the most vehement attacks on advocates of reform come from those who have benefited or hope to benefit most from the present arrangements – Ministers, Shadow Ministers in Her Majesty's Opposition, MPs who hope one day to become Shadow Ministers or Ministers – and not forgetting those other courtiers in the Palace of Westminster, the political columnists and commentators who have built careers within the system, scurrying up and down the corridors in search of gossip. Politicians, as the argot of the eighties had it, are in the business of power. No politician who wants to be a Minister is going to start advocating reforms that would limit the power of Ministers.

But perhaps this is too cynical. There is at least one argument from the Left against changing our majoritarian system of government that deserves serious consideration. This is the argument that constitutional checks and balances favour the status quo, that they give undue weight to conservative minorities and property interests, thus standing in the way of radical social and economic change. One can certainly point to American examples where constitutional checks have been used in this way. For many years in the early part of this century the US Supreme Court blocked legislation outlawing child labour. 'States's Rights' were used by whites in the South to uphold their position. These are disturbing examples, but they are a reflection more of specifically American historical circumstances than of the general experience of countries with constitutionally guaranteed rights. In Europe, Socialist governments have lived quite happily with Bills of Rights and federal systems. Clearly, it all depends in part on what general rights are guaranteed. A British Bill of Rights, for example, would be unlikely to guarantee the freedom to bear arms, as the American Constitution does. The content of a British Bill of Rights would have to be based on as broad a political consensus as possible – it could not be simply a party political measure. This is another serious flaw in the Labour Party's approach to constitutional reform: they seem to regard the four specific 'Rights' Bills as no different in kind from proposals they might put forward on, say, transport policy or taxation.

This argument from the Left for retaining parliamentary sovereignty can be expressed at a more philosophical level. Essential to Socialism is the idea of collective social action, as against the 'every-man-for-himself' philosophy of Thatcherism. Once you start giving blocking powers to minority groups, or even individuals, you destroy all chance of the collective action that is necessary to achieve radical social change. This is the argument that Lenin used against 'bourgeois democracy', and one can hear it echoed in surprising quarters in today's Labour Party. Roy Hattersley transforms himself into a Bolshevik once he gets going on the evils of Bills of Rights.

But should we equate 'collective action' solely with the actions of the state, and see Socialism merely as a collection of policies that will be 'implemented' once the machinery of the state is captured (either by revolution or election)? There are in fact signs of a new thinking on the Left (though not within the British Labour Party) that places less emphasis on the state and more on other forms of community and diversified methods of democratic control. Unlike the old statist conceptions of Socialism, these new ideas are an extension of, rather than in opposition to, pluralist, 'bourgeois' democracy. This, for example, is how the American radical activist Michael Harrington saw the future, shortly before his death last year:

> The political, social and economic development of modern society points socialism towards an ethical, multiclass, and decentralized conception of its goal based on the democratization of the workplace and the creation of new forms of community, both within the nation and throughout the world. That vision has a remarkable continuity with the basic republican values that derive from both the French and the American revolutions.

Harrington is surely right. The massive rejection by the people of Central and Eastern Europe of their Communist rulers has discredited once and for all the statist conception of Socialism. In the

West, the important political ideas of recent times – environmentalism, the women's movement, the peace movement – have come from outside the mass political parties which compete for power at the state level. As in Eastern Europe, it is 'civil society' – the network of voluntary organisations below the level of the state – that must be the focus for a new democratic politics, protected from the dead, unifying hand of central control. (One recalls Mrs Thatcher's revealingly Stalinist remark that 'there is no such thing as society'.) During the democratic revolutions in the autumn of 1989, one word that cropped up frequently in the demands of opposition groups was 'pluralism'. One can be sure that they did not have in mind anything akin to the Westminster model of two ideological dinosaurs battling for supreme power.

The idea that under a written constitution the will of the majority would be thwarted by a reactionary minority tends to take the form of the Reactionary Judges Argument (RJA) – the thesis that with a written constitution, Britain would be effectively ruled by a bunch of unrepresentative, conservative old judges rather than by a democratically elected parliament. It is certainly true that, at present, judges tend to be drawn from a narrow section of society (white, male, upper middle class) and that some of them are given to expressing strange views. One would hardly relish the prospect of Judge

Pickles becoming Chief Justice of a British Supreme Court. But for the Labour Party to deploy the RJA against the whole idea of a written constitution is somewhat disingenuous. If judges are so reactionary and unrepresentative, then the Labour Party should be bringing forward proposals for a thorough overhaul of the way in which judges are recruited, selected and trained. Indeed they should be doing this *quite apart* from the issue of constitutional reform. If these proposals were adequate, then the RJA would no longer apply. Labour and Conservative alike argue against a written constitution that the judiciary should not be dragged into politics. But the truth is that – particularly in cases involving public order and terrorism – judges already make political decisions. The only difference with a written constitution would be that the criteria for making those judgements would be stated and open to public discussion.

Proposals for a Bill of Rights are often met with the response that to suggest such things is to misunderstand utterly the nature of our country, our constitution and our political system. Here again we see that familiar circular argument: parliamentary sovereignty and an unwritten constitution should not cease to be the British way of doing things because – well, because they are the British way of doing things. Parliament somehow embodies Britishness, it is the essence of *British* democracy and freedom. Our political system is more than simply an institutional arrangement for establishing democratic control and accountability – it is the distillation of the national character. Here is Enoch Powell: 'The House of Commons is the personification of the people of Britain: its supremacy is synonymous with their self-government and freedom. Through the centuries Britain has created the House of Commons and the House of Commons has moulded Britain, until the history of the one and the life of the one cannot be separated from the history and life of the other.' Here is Michael Foot: 'It is party politics which, over a period of nearly three centuries, has provided the distinctive flavour and vitality of British freedom.' This is the kind of sentimental windbaggery that passes for debate among Great Parliamentarians. (The modern party system is not much more than a hundred years old – in that respect Foot is plain wrong.) What is *British* freedom? Does it come stamped with a Union Jack? Could a South African Minister or Chilean general, equally, talk about 'South African' or 'Chilean' freedom, each with their own 'distinctive flavour and vitality' (and hence, presumably, difficult for foreigners to understand)? Tony Benn also equates the House of Commons with 'the nation' when he describes constitutional reform (which, for him, means the Commons shaking off the shackles of the House of Lords, the Monarchy and the 'economic imperialism' of the European Community) as 'a national liberation struggle' analogous to the Third World national liberation struggles that threw off the shackles of British imperialism.

Behind these identifications of the British people with the single institution of parliament lies an assumption about the unity and undifferentiated nature of 'the British'. We have seen how the majoritarian version of democracy is rooted in the nostalgic vision of a small, homogeneous community. The doctrine of parliamentary sovereignty, in a similar way, is based on the idea that the British are 'one people', moulded together by class (in the Left version) or race (in the Right version). On this basic idea there is a remarkable congruence between the 'Albion' school of British Socialists and right-wing defenders of parliamentary sovereignty. In the career of Enoch Powell we see how the three issues that have formed his obsessions – parliamentary sovereignty (particularly as against the encroachment of the European Community), immigration (i.e. race), and Ulster unionism – come together in the idea of nationhood. They are, for him, one issue.

But British society is not (and never has been) unitary and homogeneous. The truth is that Britain has always been enormously diverse, made up of shifting and overlapping linguistic, religious, national, cultural and ethnic groups. The assertion that we are 'one people', that there is a national 'essence', has always been a lie used to justify the unjust dominance of one group (whites, Protestants, or Anglo-Saxons, for example) over the society as a whole. With our ever greater ties to continental Europe, Britain will clearly be increasingly cosmopolitan. But our political system as it stands is insensitive to this diversity. Not until the archaic structure of parliamentary sovereignty is swept away will Britain be able to come to terms with its future as a multi-national, multi-cultural society.

The argument over what makes a political system more, or less, democratic, necessarily leads to the question of British 'identity'. To cling to the doctrine of parliamentary sovereignty is to cling to an exclusive, unitary and insular conception of our identity that is irrelevant to the world in which we actually live. But that conception of our 'national identity', that whole baggage of mythology about 'our island race', still has some grip on the minds of politicians and public. Clearly there are residual memories of Empire – and hence of the myths of racial unity and superiority that were Empire's justification – in, for example, the institution of the Monarchy. But much more important, even fifty years later, is the role of the Second World War – and, in particular, of that *annus mirabilis*, 1940 – in national mythology. It is, of course, the losing sides in wars that traditionally undergo subsequent soul-searching and self-examination. For the victors, once the immediate human loss has faded, the historical events take on a rosy hue. But we should not let that nostalgic glow blind us to the true costs of the war. Economic historians, of course, have long pointed out the material costs, the way in which the war accelerated a pre-existent decline. But there were more invisible costs, too. The defence of Britain in 1940 and throughout the war *was* a miracle of national unity and mobilisation of resources, but that achievement had its dark side in a strengthened ethos of insularity and xenophobia. That ethos has persisted in the postwar years. Politicians appeal to it when, in defending parliamentary sovereignty against the encroachment of the European Community, they invoke Dunkirk and the image of Britain 'standing alone' against the rest of Europe. This siege mentality has lingered too long in the British psyche.

But it would be a mistake to think that our present political system is firmly entrenched in the sentiments of British people. The conception of 'national identity' outlined above has taken a considerable battering over the past twenty-five years with the resurgence of Celtic nationalisms, the demands of multi-racialism and, above all, the realisation that the only possible future for Britain lies in closer ties with the rest of Europe. More generally, there is considerable disenchantment (if ever there really was much enchantment) with Westminster itself. It remains to be seen whether the televising of parliament will alleviate or exacerbate that. The only people who maintain veneration for the place, who keep alive the pompous mythology of 'Great Parliamentary Occasions' (the title of a book by Powell), are men who have spent most of their adult lives closeted there. Among the wider public, cynicism about our democratic institutions and the value of a vote is common, and not altogether unfounded. According to a 1986 opinion poll, 71 per cent of people questioned said that a Bill of Rights would increase their confidence in British democracy. This discontent with our political system has yet to be articulated or to make itself felt in the political arena. But this may yet change. In the autumn of 1988, a popular campaign was formed, 'Charter 88', calling for a Bill of Rights, a written constitution, proportional representation and regional assemblies – calling, in short, for a move away from our majoritarian system of parliamentary sovereignty towards something more pluralistic. Charter 88 – like the green and women's movements – has its origins outside the world of Westminster politics. Already, as we have seen, the Labour Party has been forced to at least give itself the appearance of responding. The Liberals, of course, have been advocating electoral and constitutional reform for years.

In the early part of this century, writers on the Left like G.D.H. Cole and Harold Laski criticised the whole idea of 'sovereignty', and called for more pluralistic political systems. Although the First World War gave the nation-state a bad name, there appeared to be an element of wishful thinking, of utopianism, in their demands. Today, the situation is quite different. Reform of our political system is not only desirable, in that it would make it more democratic – it is also realistic, in that Europe is clearly moving in the direction of a greater diversity of forms of democratic control and accountability. Power is being diffused away from the level of the nation-state – upward to supranational bodies, and downward to regions. This process raises new problems – how, for example, to democratise the European Community by strengthening the European Parliament as against the Council of Ministers. But to cling to the idea that power should continue to be concentrated exclusively at the level of the nation-state is to ignore these genuine problems of democracy posed by the new Europe.

These are problems that face the whole of Europe, but in the British case – because of the way our political system concentrates power in the hands of one party in parliament – they are posed in an acute and distinct form. Looking at the list of eight 'majoritarian' characteristics of our political system outlined above, it may seem that we are facing an edifice so ossified and rigid that it would be impossible to reform it. I have deliberately taken a broad approach – rather than concentrating exclusively on, say, a Bill of Rights or proportional representation – in order to suggest that there is something wrong with the whole political culture, rather than a few minor faults that could be put right by reform around the edges, or simply by a change of government. It clearly would be utopian to expect the whole system to change at once. The one immediate reform that, politically, could break this current deadlock, clearing the way for other changes, is proportional representation. Labour has allowed the possibility of their proposed second chamber being elected by PR – which immediately raises the question: if for one chamber, why not the other?

In the future, we need to escape from the idea that democracy should consist merely of a game of electoral roulette played once every five years. We need to think instead of the different levels of democratic control, accountability and representation that different areas of human activity demand. Education, law and order, cultural policy, could be decided at a more local level. Environmental matters and the increasingly globalised industrial and commercial sectors can only be regulated and democratically controlled at a supranational level. Somewhere within this spectrum there would continue to be a place for Westminster. But it must cease to hold that monopoly of power which currently exerts such a paralysing influence on our society.

The new international debate about democracy is only just beginning. We in Britain may yet learn important lessons from the struggles for a democratic reconstruction of society in Central and Eastern Europe. But whatever the source, we do need a new democratic constitution in this country. We need it both to protect the freedoms that are essential to democracy and to ensure that sectarian, divisive measures like the poll tax cannot be forced into law against the wishes of vast numbers of people.

The following books are quoted or have been particularly useful in writing this pamphlet:

Tony Benn, *Arguments for Democracy* (Penguin, 1982)

B.W. Hill (ed), *Edmund Burke on Government, Politics and Society* (Fontana, 1975)

Robert A. Dahl, *Democracy and its Critics* (Yale University Press, 1989)

A.V. Dicey, *Introduction to the Study of the Law of the Constitution* (Macmillan, 7th ed. 1908)

Charles Dickens, *Our Mutual Friend* (Penguin, 1971)

Michael Foot, *Loyalists and Loners* (Collins, 1986)

Alexander Hamilton, James Madison and John Jay, *The Federalist Papers* (New American Library, 1961)

Michael Harrington, *Socialism: Past and Future* (Little, Brown and Company, 1989)

Roy Lewis, *Enoch Powell: Principle in Politics* (Cassell, 1979)

Arend Lijphart, *Democracies* (Yale University Press, 1984)

*Political Quarterly* (Vol. 60 no. 4, Oct–Dec 1989)

Peter Thornton, *Decade of Decline: Civil Liberties in the Thatcher Years* (National Council for Civil Liberties, 1989)

I would also like to thank Diana Hinds, Jack Lively and Jonathan Burnham for their comments on an earlier draft.

# About The Author

ADAM LIVELY was born in Swansea in 1961, and studied history and philosophy in England and America. He has published two novels, *Blue Fruit* and *The Burnt House*, and has appeared in the anthologies *20 Under 35*, *P.E.N. New Poetry II* and *The Dylan Companion*. He is a tutor for the Workers' Educational Association and the Extra-Mural Studies Department of London University.

# CHATTO
# CounterBlasts

Also available in bookshops now:-

No. 1  Jonathan Raban       **God, Man & Mrs Thatcher**
No. 2  Paul Foot            **Ireland:** Why Britain Must Get Out
No. 3  John Lloyd           **A Rational Advance for the
                            Labour Party**
No. 4  Fay Weldon           **Sacred Cows:** A Portrait of Britain,
                            post-Rushdie, pre-Utopia
No. 5  Marina Warner        **Into the Dangerous World**
No. 6  William Shawcross    **Kowtow!**
No. 7  Ruth Rendell and     **Undermining the Central Line**
       Colin Ward
No. 8  Mary Warnock         **Universities:** Knowing Our Minds
No. 9  Sue Townsend         **Mr Bevan's Dream**
No. 10 Christopher          **The Monarchy**
       Hitchens
No. 11 Tessa Blackstone     **Prisons and Penal Reform**
No. 12 Douglas Dunn         **Poll Tax: The Fiscal Fake**
No. 13 Ludovic Kennedy      **Euthanasia**
No. 14 Adam Mars-Jones      **Venus Envy**

### Forthcoming Chatto CounterBlasts

No. 16 Margaret Drabble     **Safe as Houses**
No. 17 Ronald Dworkin       **A Bill of Rights for Britain**

Plus pamphlets from Michael Holroyd, Hanif Kureishi, Michael
Ignatieff and Susannah Clapp

If you want to join in the debate, and if you want to know more about
**CounterBlasts**, the writers and the issues, then write to:

Random Century Group, Freepost 5066, Dept MH, London SW1V
2YY